TRAVELING THROUGH NORTH KOREA

ADVENTURES
in the
HERMIT KINGDOM

FROM THE VOICE BEHIND BIGBEAVERDIARIES.COM
STEPHEN HARRIS

Tellwell Talent

www.tellwell.ca

ISBN

978-1-77370-614-6 (Paperback)

TABLE OF CONTENTS

Prologue: The North Korea Decision V

Crossing from China to North Korea 1

Travel in North Korea. 25

The Road 49

The North Korean Side of the DMZ 65

Back to Pyongyang 77

Kumgang, North Korea 89

Life in the DPRK. 117

A Return to the Capital 137

Exiting North Korea. 151

PROLOGUE: THE NORTH KOREA DECISION
CHINA - JUNE, 2017

Now I know what you are thinking. "Is he nuts? North Korea? Has he misplaced the small amount of sanity he had?" At the risk of stealing from the drama, the answer is "No." It may seem that I often do things that are dangerous. But the truth is that this is not really the case. Every major decision I make has been carefully considered, thought through and researched.

> I call this decision The North Korea Decision, and in this situation, the timing of the trip to North Korea would be the biggest hiccup.

How did it get to this, you wonder?

Well, The North Korea Decision began about five weeks earlier in Prague, Czech Republic, when I was having a post-birthday hangover breakfast with two friends. They were asking about places I had been and asked if I had visited North Korea.

I had been asked this question so many times that I decided that I needed to have a better answer...

At that moment at the table, I took out my phone and researched flights to Beijing, knowing that China was the only access point to North Korea. I found a flight from Prague to Beijing for £276. £276! Cheap! That is $360! Then I looked up tours into North Korea as I knew that a guided tour was the only way that a visit to North Korea could take place. I thought it was going to be a couple of thousand dollars, but instead I found tours for about $800. That was also much cheaper than I expected. The North Korea Decision had been made. I decided I would go.

(*Note:* Keep in mind that all of this took place before the major events surrounding the coma, release and death of Otto Warmbier. More on all of that later...)

The trip took me from Prague to Greece to meet a Canadian friend; Greece to Egypt to see the pyramids; Egypt to Thailand to meet a Scottish friend; Thailand to Taiwan to surprise an American friend; Taiwan to China by ferry, and then transportation to a city in China next to North Korea called Dandong.

But, then things went awry...

I had come to Asia to see important people in my life, but my number one priority for visiting that part of the world had been to make the trip to North Korea. And then on June 14, the story of Otto Warmbier made major waves in the media.

Warmbier, of course, was the American college student who had been released by North Korean authorities and sent back to the US in a coma state after 17 months of North Korean detention for stealing a poster from a hotel. Warmbier had originally been sentenced to 15 years of hard labor, but had been in a coma for the past year. His release set the internet ablaze and, to be honest, I had never even heard of the young man until he was being sent home.

> The story of Warmbier's release happened 10 days before I was planning to enter North Korea.
>
> I realized it was really bad timing. The problem was that I was already in China. Had these circumstances happened a month earlier, I would have likely pulled the plug on my decision to visit North Korea.
>
> I spent some time researching and reading about the case. I eventually decided that I would still go.
>
> Then on June 20, just four days before I was about to go into North Korea, I got word that Warmbier had died...

After reading President Trump's response to the incident, I wondered if a war might break out. I contacted Sabrina, a Chinese local, who runs Explore North Korea Tours in Dandong, China, and told her I was extremely concerned. She calmly explained how this was an isolated incident and that nothing was going to happen to me. I was worried about being a target, and I asked her if any other westerners were going to be on the trip I was booked on. She said there were none—I was the only one.

I started to back off, but Sabrina calmly assured me that there would be plenty of other westerners in North Korea at the time I would be there. Several westerners would be staying in the hotel where I was booked. She told me that she regularly travels to North Korea with her family, and they do not think about sensitive political issues. She said that, instead, they worry about whether or not they have packed enough traditional food.

> I was pretty uncomfortable with the whole situation.
> The timing and the stories in the media could not have
> been any worse.

I decided I would at least head to the China/North Korea border city of Dandong to meet Sabrina to discuss The North Korea Decision. Since I already had my plane and train tickets booked to get me to Dandong, I figured I might as well use them to have a face-to-face meeting with her to feel out the situation.

So, I arrived in Dandong, China, on the 23rd, the day before my tour was to begin. I took Sabrina out for lunch. We had a long discussion, and she walked me through everything. She promised me that there would not be any issues. She told me that North Korea is a beautiful country and that the people are amazing. I told her that the money she could make from me was not worth my life. Her demeanor was calm and her eyes were honest when she told me that everything would be fine. She assured me that it is normal to have concerns, but that I really would be okay.

> I put a lot of value into a person's eyes, as they provide
> a lot of information. It is often that I bank on eyes
> in situations to be certain that people are sincere.
> I trusted her and I decided that I would go.

Now, it is very unfortunate what happened to Otto Warmbier. In reality, he did something very foolish, got caught and paid the heaviest price possible for a bad decision. I myself have made plenty of poor decisions late at night in foreign lands, but I have managed to dodge any serious consequences. People know that about my personality, so I only told three people where and when I was going. All three of the people who knew of my trip were concerned about my behavior. I assured them all that I could behave. I needed to. Perhaps the trip could even teach me something about humility and normality...

I sometimes think that Warmbier's terrible fate may have been a serious advantage to my own life. Perhaps it saved my own life. His fate assured that I would toe the line in a way I probably would not have without knowing his story. Warmbier's fate made me behave.

I would head into North Korea the following morning...

CROSSING FROM CHINA TO NORTH KOREA
DAY 1—PART I

Dandong, China

Disclaimer: You probably want to read about how scary and frightening it was to cross from China into North Korea to spend some days in the Hermit Kingdom. You probably want to hear how dangerous it was and the terror I felt every minute that I was in the country.
It was nothing like that.
It was nothing you would ever imagine.
A trip to North Korea is a very special experience.

I was up at 06:30 to get ready for my five-day/four-night trip to North Korea. I had a list of jobs to work on, including going onto my website and taking down any articles that were connected to politics or political events. Also, I removed any recent stories to make Big Beaver Diaries seem dormant. Then I temporarily deactivated my personal Facebook page and my Big Beaver Diaries Facebook page. There was no point in taking chances. The risks in North Korea seemed minute, but if I could dial down my media presence, I might as well... just in case.

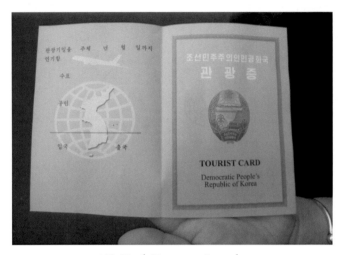

My North Korean tourist card.

I was at the Dandong train station at 08:30 to meet Sabrina from Explore North Korea Tours. She was there waiting for our group and I was the first to arrive. There would be seven Chinese nationals heading into North Korea with me on the tour.

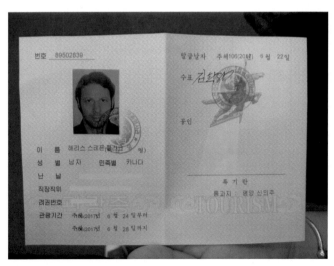

My North Korea tourist visa! My options were to receive it like this or as a stamp in my passport. The former seemed like the obvious choice to avoid raised eyebrows from officials in other nations.

For my crossing from China to North Korea, I had left my entire luggage in storage at the train station with the exception of four clean pairs of underwear, four pairs of socks, three shirts, a pair of shorts, and whatever I was already wearing.

Oh, I also had two celebratory cigars purchased in Egypt.
That was all I took, in addition to a couple of pens and a small notepad from Portugal.
No phone.
No laptop.
I was not taking any chances.

I did not even have my own camera because mine has GPS on it and that is not allowed in North Korea.
Luckily, Sabrina had a small, outdated point-and-shoot Canon camera which she loaned me for the trip.
My photos would not be great, but at least I would have photos. The camera she handed me was pink.
The more I thought about it, the more insignificant I was... a westerner without much more than vital bits of clothing, a notepad, a couple of pens, and a pink outdated camera.

Sabrina could only follow me so far into the Dandong train station, and then I was left with the Chinese tourists who could not speak English. She told one of them to take care of me until we got to Pyongyang, North Korea. My English-speaking guide would be waiting at the Pyongyang train station for me and would take charge from there.

North Korea-bound bananas, apples and luggage.

The North Koreans, identifiable by their red nationality pins on their chests with images of Kim Il-sung and Kim Jong-il, were heading through immigration with the Chinese tourists. The North Koreans had boxes of bananas and boxes of apples, fruit they have no access to in their own country. We were all standing in a huge room waiting to check out of China through Chinese immigration. I was the only white guy in a room of about 1,000 humans. I was handed someone's luggage to bring through immigration. That made me very uncomfortable in my North American mindset of a typical airport-loudspeaker warning "Never Carry Anyone Else's Luggage" blaring at an uncomfortable volume in my head. I knew it was probably harmless, but after a couple of minutes I casually traded the luggage back to the same man for a bag that contained our pre-organized train lunches.

Looking around at the other tourists, I noticed that I was about three decades younger than the majority and the least likely to require hip-replacement surgery in the next five years. Also, the Chinese do not dye their hair blue when they reach a certain age as elderly North American women are wont to do. It is mystifying to me that one culture appears to eschew Elderly Blue, while another embraces it...

4

That, you can be assured, is a hangover-sleep on the train...

After quickly clearing Chinese exit-immigration, my group ascended to our assigned section of a stationary train. The train started to move across the nearly one-kilometer Friendship Bridge between China and North Korea and we pulled into a North Korean town called Sinuiju. That bridge is the crossing from China to North Korea.

My first view of North Korea. They look like they are having fun. Wait? Fun is allowed in North Korea? What?

The train stopped at the station and North Korean immigration officials in light brown uniforms and hats were everywhere outside of our train windows. I was nervous. Why was I nervous? Likely due to the media. I have spoken with so many immigration officials in my life that there was no reason for me to be nervous, but this circumstance made me very uneasy.

The Chinese man who seemed to feel "in charge" of me motioned that I should get out my passport when the others got out theirs. I actually did not need him to show me what to do—I may not have spoken the same language, but I do have something of a sense of perception.

Immigration officials boarded the train. In our train car, we were in sections of six with rows of bunk beds stacked three high. An official made his way to our section.

> I was expecting stern no-nonsense faces. The official smiled at us. I attracted a lot of attention from the locals and the tourists because I am a westerner. I was *the* westerner. The official came close to me, looked at my passport cover, and said, "Ah, Canada!" in a gentle voice.

That was my first interaction with a North Korean. He immediately helped me feel more relaxed. The official was nothing like I had imagined a North Korean official would be. He exuded a warm aura. He searched my bag with barely a look. I could have smuggled puppies into his country! It was not the strict and regimented bag search that I had been warned about.

The immigration official asked for my phone, but I was without one. The women in my section were scanned by a female official with a metal detector. I was passed over by the officials doing the metal detector search for some reason...

The North Korean badge on our train.

After all of our passports were taken in a giant stack, opened to our photo page by the official, we disembarked from the train in the station where two trolleys of snacks and goods were being sold by North Korean girls in white blouses, distinct black skirts and individually stylish high-heeled shoes. I had not been expecting variations of anything—just different sizes of brown slacks and shoes in the communist country.

I had previously read somewhere that the prettiest girls are chosen to work such jobs to create a good first impression. These girls were doing just that! In addition to Chinese and North Korean snacks, they were also selling German and Czech beer. On my *Top Ten Things I Have Zero Interest in Doing while in North Korea*, drinking beer from Germany or the Czech Republic was certainly on the list.

Glam shot of dried fish for $1.

One of the Chinese girls from my section bought an entire dried fish for the equivalent of $1. We had a great time taking glam shots with that fish and time passed in a hurry. When our passports returned with the same official about 20 minutes later, everyone got back on the train. The official went to hand my passport back and said, "Meesta Canada!" to me with a smile. It was nice. My previous stereotypes were seriously being challenged, and I had only been in the country for a grand total of half an hour.

> I was not expecting any humor or personality when dealing with North Korean border agents on my crossing from China to North Korea.

The train eventually departed the station and we headed deep into North Korea. In actuality, I had more difficulty getting a Chinese visa and passing through immigration to get into China than I did getting a North Korean visa and passing through immigration to get into the Democratic People's Republic of Korea.

There were three young Chinese girls on the trip who were about my age. I befriended them and got to learn that the $880 I had spent on a five-day/four-night trip was only $370 had I been Chinese and would have been on a four-day/three-night trip instead. That seems like quite a tricky amount of money for one extra day... I blame my passport. Living and learning...

North Korean rice paddies.

The first thing to really grab me as the train headed out on the four-hour trip towards the North Korean capital of Pyongyang, was that there were no roads anywhere which also meant that there were no cars. Rice paddies cover the land as far as the eye can see in every direction. The paddies are built up with an intelligent system where they are terraced and irrigated from rivers within the country. The water flows through the paddies and down to the next level of paddies terraced below. Man-made channels/trenches bring the water in to the paddies, often from many miles away, and the water is distributed so that the paddies are constantly saturated to make the rice grow.

Crossing the rice paddy boundary paths.

Farmers dot the fields to maintain the crops, and the field boundaries—built up to control water flow—act as walkways between plots. Often there are people on bikes riding along these narrow passages. The paddies are in the open countryside, yet there are people everywhere.

The white rocks have pesticides on them to keep the bugs away from the freshly planted trees. Local gatherings in the countryside shade are a common sight.

Initial Observations About North Korea:

★ Occasionally there would be a large truck on a dusty path moving something (or a load of locals in the back) somewhere.

★ The fields would often have farmers working the land with oxen and a one-bottom wooden plow. Sometimes instead of oxen, there would be an old tractor with steel wheels designed for driving through the muddy rice paddies.

★ Seeing a military tank on a cargo train as it is being moved across the country is a startling sight.

★ The North Korean rail hostess girls were pushing carts of snacks and beer through the train cars where we were seated. After about five passes, and me smiling at them every time, one of them winked at me. I expected them to be so shy, and this girl surprised me so much that I started giggling like a teenager.

★ When our train tracks would cross the occasional road, there would always be a soldier standing at the crossing. Also, the arm that went across the road—to keep the non-existent traffic from coming though—was a wooden pole painted red and white. Sometimes the poles would be crooked and out of shape.

★ At some point, our train passed a monument where two sculpted bears wearing boxing gloves were sparring against each other.

★ The North Korean landscape is spotlessly clean. This is unlike most other Asian nations, where plastic bags and plastic bottles are strewn everywhere.

Bicycles on the road to somewhere.

I was initially quite nervous about writing in a notepad on the train. The application form for a visa to visit North Korea stated that "journalists were not allowed to apply." Paranoia that I could be seen as some sort of western spy crept in during the train ride. However, there were so many things that I wanted to write down about what I was seeing and feeling in the initial experience.

Pulling in to Pyongyang. The colors of the city are magnificent.
I had been expecting everything to be gray.

12

I had also taken a few photos, but I was edgy doing this as well. It felt like there were North Korean eyes on me when I would pull out my camera, just waiting to tell the government that there was a suspicious western man on the train with a notepad and a pink camera! So, I actually went into the toilet on the train with my notepad to furiously scribble down some memory-trigger words about the experience. Eventually, I loosened up and got comfortable jotting down notes or clicking my camera, but primarily, this was not the case. Not the case at all...

Pulling in to the train station in Pyongyang, North Korea.

When the train eventually pulled in to Pyongyang and I disembarked, a young North Korean man approached me and asked, "Are you from Canada?"

"Yes, I am," I replied with suspicion.

"My name is Kim, and I am your North Korea guide."

"Oh... good..."

A FEW MORE PHOTOS OF
CROSSING FROM CHINA
TO NORTH KOREA:

My first sighting of Kim Il-sung and Kim Jong-il.

Locals busing their way through Sinuiju, North Korea.

Look at the age of that ride. Continuous fun since the 1940s!

Colorful North Korean countryside housing flats.

Saturated rice paddies and tractors with steel wheels designed for the mud.

North Korean rice paddies.

There are people everywhere in the middle of nowhere in North Korea.

Typical North Korean farming village.

*Locals, hanging out. They are probably smoking cigarettes
while waiting for the tractor-trailer!*

The beautiful age of that tractor, the smoke and the riders in the wagon...

Our train ride through North Korea.

The train toilet. Straight down and onto the tracks below.

The North Korean train hostess girls, tired from a long day.
There are three of them sleeping at their tables.

Storage on the fields.

Harvest taking place.

Dadong Gang, the most common beer in North Korea.

Farmers working the fields as a team.

TRAVEL IN NORTH KOREA
DAY I—PART 2

Pyongyang, DPRK

Since I was the only English speaker on the trip, I would have my own personal guide while the Chinese tourists would share theirs. The first thing that Kim, my assigned North Korean guide, did at the train station was ask to have my passport for his own keeping during my visit. He said it was his job to keep it and me safe. That seemed strangely controlling, but his tone offered no choice in the matter so I slowly and uncomfortably handed it over while looking him in the eye. Kim, 28 years old, tucked it away in a shoulder bag he was wearing. I then decided not to make fun of his shoulder bag as I had originally planned upon meeting him. The guy would be carrying my passport inside of that man-bag...

Arriving at the train station in Pyongyang, North Korea.

Kim would be by my side no matter what I was doing for the next five days from morning until evening as I would travel through North Korea. My guide was the last face I would see before I went to bed and the first person I would greet in the morning once I headed downstairs for breakfast. Kim would provide information and an explanation for everything.

My first steps into Pyongyang, North Korea. It is a city of pastel colors.

Some North Korean Details:

★ *The population of North Korea, also known as the Democratic People's Republic of Korea (DPRK), is 20 million people.*

★ *Pyongyang, the capital, has a population of 2.5 million.*

★ *There are hardly any cars in the streets of clean and quiet Pyongyang. Think of your own city at 04:00; that same amount of traffic is the equivalent of rush hour in Pyongyang. There has never been a traffic jam in the history of time in Pyongyang.**

★ *The leaders of DPRK since 1945 have been "President" Kim Il-sung (1956-1994), succeeded by his son, "Chairman" Kim Jong-il (1994-2011), succeeded by his son, "Marshal" Kim Jong-un (2012 to present).*

★ *I made a reference to Kim Il-sung, and Kim immediately corrected me with, "President, Kim Il-sung." I was careful not to make the same mistake again so I would not offend my guide.*

★ *The Korean War began on June 25, 1950, and the current ceasefire began on July 27, 1953.*

★ *DPRK is, of course, a dictatorship to the foreign eye, but to the North Koreans, it is governed by the Workers' Party of Korea. The symbols for the WPK are a calligraphy brush for the intellectual, a hammer for the worker, and a sickle for the farmer.*

★ *Kim told me that the only rules for me would be: a) I could not take photos of any soldiers in North Korea (this would prove to be difficult as they are everywhere all of the time) and b) I would have to ask permission from any civilians if I wanted a photo of them.*

* The traffic jam detail is an observed guess... as is the rush-hour traffic reference!

*Children enjoying themselves after school at Grand
People's Study House and Fountain Park.*

*Note: Now, I had made the decision upon entering North Korea that I was going there to see
what they wanted to show me. Of course I would have loved to have gone off the barely-beaten
path, but that would not be an option, so I was there to see their "presentation." I had decided
to take it in just as it was shown to me. There could be incorrect information through some of
this, but what I am writing is North Korea through the eyes of a North Korean as presented
to a foreigner, and North Korea as my eyes saw it with very little previous information. I was
there to take it all in as it is and as it looks.*

*There is a lot of color flavor in Pyongyang. The only grays are the
unfinished buildings. The 105-story, 330-meter pyramid-shaped
unfinished Ryugyong Hotel looms in the background.*

28

We were loaded onto a bus and driven around the city. I was amazed by the appearance of Pyongyang. When I decided to travel North Korea, I was expecting a typical gray and communist-looking city. It is not that at all. The city is full of very tall apartment buildings, and all of them are painted. The skyline is made up of blues, yellows, greens, reds, pinks, oranges... everything has a color. Pyongyang is the most colorful city I have seen in the world outside of Latin America.

My seven-year-old English-speaking pals.

Our first stop was Fountain Park where two children walking along were smiling at me. I said, "Hello!" to them. One of the boys replied, "Hello, how are you?" The other asked, "What is your name?" I was amazed they spoke English. Kim told me that English is now the second language of North Korea. English is more important than Chinese or Russian.

Kim Il-sung Square. You can see photos of Kim Il-sung and Kim Jong-il on the building.

We made a stop at Kim Il-sung Square where important functions take place. There were slogans on the tops of the buildings that said, "Long Live the Workers' Party of Korea" and "Long Live DPRK" in Korean. Our next visit was to the Grand People's Study House where Kim told me there is a book in every language of the world. I took his word, but that sure does seem suspect...

Tower of Juche Idea by day.

Tower of Juche Idea by night.

Finally, we made our way to the Tower of the Juche Idea. My guide told me that Juche is the official state ideology and roughly translates to "The capacity to shape our destiny." That is nice. I was told that the Tower of the Juche Idea is the tallest stone structure in the world at 170 meters high, 20 meters of which are the flame on the top.

Once Kim and I had been together for about an hour, I began to ask him about his life. He told me that in DPRK:

★ *The government gives a couple free housing once they are married. There are never bills or rent to pay.*

★ *The bigger the family, the bigger the house. Should you want a bigger home to live in, have another child and expand your whole life. A bigger family equals a better house.*

★ *Education is all free in DPRK. Want to be a doctor? Want to be a plumber? It is all free to study.*

★ *All healthcare is free for life. DPRK healthcare includes dentistry.*

★ *Vouchers or "food stamps" are allotted for meat, rice, eggs and cloth.*

★ *Kim told me everyone is also allotted vouchers that entitle them to one free liter a beer each day...* *

(Insert your own mental record-scratch sound here!)

... Now just think about that for a second. One liter of beer a day. If you saved them all for Saturday, you would have enough tickets for 14 different 500ml beers every week. Imagine if you did not do anything for a month. That would be 60 of them. Now, how about it you went two months without going out and you had 120 tickets for 500ml of beer? Imagine the party you could throw? You could invite everyone you knew and tell them to invite their friends, as well. People you do not even know could crash your pad

and you would be able to happily supply them with a free party. This beer-ticket rationing system seems pretty good to me...

I asked Kim if anyone has long hair like mine. He told me, "No. It is not our tradition. Short-haired people are called 'smart.' People with long hair, 'not smart.'" I could see where this was going. I decided I would play the fool for the tour. Smart people end up getting themselves into trouble anyhow...

Everyone loaded onto the bus and we were taken to a restaurant where there were two big beer bottles on each table for every four seats. We had been combined with another Chinese tour group and there was another young guy in our group named Wu Zheng Yu. Wu Zheng Yu and I drank all of the beer at the table. *All* of the beer...

I am not sure if Wu Zheng Yu knew what he was getting into when he decided that he would be my partner in crime, but we put back a lot of lager. Wu Zheng Yu eventually stopped cheers-ing me when he realized I would drink my entire glass after the "clink" and he felt obliged to follow suit...

Somewhere along the way, Wu Zheng Yu realized that I was trouble...

The pre-organized fancy restaurant in Pyongyang
where we would dine on our initial night.

I made a lot of friends quickly at the dinner table. Perhaps that was in part because of the effort I made for everyone that I was sitting with. I made all of the Chinese people around me write down their names in my notebook and tried hard to remember how to pronounce them. It made me shine in their eyes.

> People in other cultures really appreciate it when you make a genuine effort to know who they are.

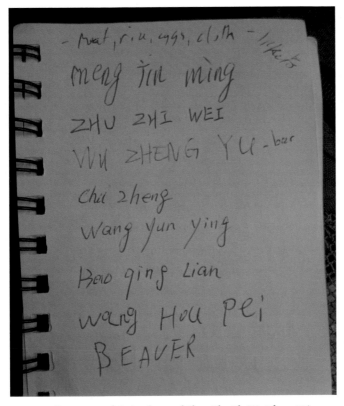

My dinner gang. (Notice the word "beer" beside Wu Zheng Yu's name so I would remember which one belonged to him.)

As dinner wrapped up, a North Korean guide approached me and asked in Spanish where I was from. I had told Kim earlier that my second-best language is Spanish, but I speak similar to a three-year-old—a very young three-year-old. Kim mentioned this to a Spanish-speaking North Korean guide, and when he started speaking to me, I had a hard time putting my brain into Spanish gear. The language sort of blindsided me and I was extremely unprepared to try to speak it. I was in North Korea and a local was speaking Spanish to me... It was so strange that it took me a moment to even be able to respond. The guide told me that he gets about 10 Spanish tourists each year. He learned the language in university, just as Kim had learned English with thoughts of working in international business before the idea of being a tour guide entered his mind.

Inside the Yanggakdo International Hotel. High-end!

The bus took us to our home for three of the next four nights: the Yanggakdo International Hotel. Kim told me it was not just a five-star or Michelin-starred hotel...it was in a "special class" of hotels on its own. There were two special classes of hotels in Pyongyang, and we would be staying at the best one in the city!

Relatively dark Pyongyang from my 40th-floor room.

The Yanggakdo International Hotel is 47 stories tall, and it has a revolving restaurant and bar at the top for a panoramic view of Pyongyang. I was given a room on the 40th floor to take in the city and its sights.

The hotel had a beautiful entrance and I realized it was the kind of hotel that I never stay in. Fancy chandeliers and giant fish tanks are not important to me. I am generally happy enough with a mattress that I will not catch crabs from, a door that locks, a shower with hot water, and a floor attached to the walls so that the cockroaches do not hassle my slumber too much. That's enough for me... The Yanggakdo International Hotel provided life luxury excess far beyond my needs.

Teaching Kim to smoke cigars in the 47th-floor revolving restaurant.

I took Kim and a Chinese girl named Jo to the revolving restaurant on the 47th floor where I bought them beer. The big beer bottles were a reasonable $4.50, and I smoked a cigar in celebration of my arrival.* The restaurant was the epitome of 1980s brown décor. It was awesome. When I went for a walk inside the restaurant, I found all of the staff gathered around a television watching a North Korean drama from the 1970s, though it is also possible that the drama was actually filmed last year. There is just no way to measure what is what in regards to advancements in North Korean technology...

* Of course I could smoke a cigar inside of a North Korean revolving restaurant!

Check out that telephone in my room! 1980s amazing!

> We were the last people to leave the revolving restaurant and I could not help but notice that Wu Zheng Yu did not make it up for a drink after I had invited him...

Eventually, I made my way to my room and found that only four of the eight elevators of the best hotel in Pyongyang were in working order. When I realized I was going to need water for the morning, I headed back up to the revolving restaurant and the revolving part of it had already been shut down, rendering it only a "restaurant"—and one that was about to close. North Korean power-saving thriftiness! I then realized they had been revolving the place just for my friends and I as we sat to drink beer.

Luxury 1980s rug in the Yanggakdo International Hotel.

I tried to get back to my room by taking the stairs and ended up in a strange corridor where I knew I was not allowed to be. There seemed to be costumes hanging on the walls. I had promised friends at home that I would behave while I was in North Korea, but it is hard to control my wandering spirit and it was difficult to not end up in a ridiculous costume for the entertainment of the closing restaurant staff. I know a fun opportunity when I see one! However, I was in North Korea and I knew enough to get out of the corridor, resisted temptation, and headed back to my room with best-behavior disappointment. As a lousy trade-off, I decided to go and see what North Korea offered in terms of television programming.

Television in my room in the "special class" Yanggakdo International Hotel.

It was a treat to find that there were only two channels in my room and both of them were very snowy. The first snowy channel was all about the hotel. The second channel was an English channel with news that us foreigners were allowed to see in North Korea.

The best hotel in Pyongyang... I knew this was going to be interesting...

A FEW MORE PHOTOS OF
TRAVEL IN NORTH KOREA:

Random television screen outside of the Pyongyang train station.

Fountain Park in Pyongyang.

These huts are for selling flowers to place at the bronze statues of Kim Il- sung and Kim Jong-il, but the statues were undergoing maintenance repairs and visitors were not allowed.

In the background of Fountain Park looms the unfinished, 105-story, Ryugyong Hotel, also known as the tallest unoccupied building in the world.

The symbol for the Workers' Party of Korea: a brush for the intellectuals, a hammer for the workers, and a sickle for the farmers.

The characters say, "Long Live the Workers' Party of Korea" and "Long Live DPRK."

The DPRK badge.

Dining with the Chinese, just before making Wu Zheng Yu (black shirt) over-drink.

*This taxi collection would later seem strange to me as I hardly
saw a taxi for the rest of the time I was in North Korea.*

*An amazing nightstand in my hotel. I could not pick up
any radio stations, but not for a lack of trying.*

The river running through Pyongyang and the Tower of Juche Idea to the right.

넷

THE ROAD
DAY 2-PART I

Pyongyang, DPRK

*Never would I have believed it before, but that absurdly
placed phone would come in handy...*

I received three wake-up calls this morning from 06:30 onward. No one wanted to let me sleep in. Last night I noticed there was a phone right next to the toilet in the bathroom. I found that peculiar, but it sure was convenient when my third wake-up call came as I was showering. I was able to just grab the phone in one step. Thanks special-class Yanggakdo International Hotel!

Good morning, foggy, music-playing Pyongyang!

I opened the window of my 40th floor room, and I heard classical music coming from outside somewhere. Kim would later tell me that the train station begins broadcasting music through the city from 06:00.

Awesome.

The Yanggakdo International Hotel. I slept up there somewhere on the 40th of 47 floors. The revolving restaurant sits at the top, but concludes rotating once my friends and I finish drinking beer for the evening. It seems to be indicative of importance!

After breakfast, we loaded onto the bus and drove through Pyongyang on our way to the Demilitarized Zone (DMZ) between North and South Korea. We passed by Mirae Scientists Street, a street in the city that was built entirely in 2016.

> When I say *built entirely*, I am not just talking about the pavement, I am talking about the buildings as well!

There were at least forty brand-new, colorful, massive apartment buildings lining the giant street, which were built to house the intellects, lecturers and teachers from one of the universities nearby. All built in 2016. All built by soldiers. It is an impressive feat to construct something on such a grand scale so quickly.

Mirae Scientists Street. Oh, but there is more, way more...

The North Koreans love to talk about how much they can get done in a short amount of time. I asked my guide Kim how fast the street went up and how many soldiers he thought were involved. Kim told me that there were major changes to the street every single day, and if he was to guess, there were probably 50,000 soldiers working on its construction. Once it was completed, the soldiers went back to their regular roles in the military.

As we drove along, hundreds of military soldiers in yellow hard hats were making their way to work in single file.

No big deal. The entire street and ALL of the buildings were constructed last year. Power in numbers...

As we left the city it was unpleasant to find that the road from Pyongyang to Kaesong, at the bottom of North Korea, was *incredibly* rough. You might think you know rough roads, but you do not know "North Korea Rough." It was tricky business to try to get photos through the bus window that did not turn out to be incredibly blurry.

One of my favorite photos from North Korea. The non-blurry edition.

53

The bus bounced and launched itself through dips, holes and cracks for the next three hours to get us to the DMZ. My guide, Kim, told me that I could have a nap if I wanted while we were driving through the country. I am not sure how he expected me to do that—I was having a hard enough time concentrating on staying in my seat without being bounced off the side windows. Maybe I am a non-conformist, but I have always found it difficult to fall asleep on a roller-coaster track camouflaged as a highway.

On top of that, a North Korean Chinese-speaking female guide had the bus microphone. For an hour straight she went on and on about North Korean/Chinese relations in something resembling a yell-talk. It was a a solid 10 on *The 10-Scale of Awful Rides*. I am certain that the front tires of the bus came off the highway on at least three occasions.

Kids really enjoying the day.

There were essentially no other cars on the road. There were many bicycles around, and the occasional motorcycle, but for the most part, the roads in North Korea are empty except for the locals walking along them. It is quite likely that many people in the country have never actually been inside of an automobile in their lives.

Desolation. Make that, rough desolation. I hadn't noticed the soldier in the photo until after I took it. I showed it to Kim, and he was concerned as the soldier being in the image technically makes this an illegal photo.

Subsequently, it is bizarre when, suddenly, in the middle of the sparse countryside, there will be infrastructure in the form of a clover-leaf overpass to change from the main road to a smaller road heading off in a perpendicular direction. If you just stopped and turned left across the oncoming traffic lane onto another road, the odds of you having to deal with other traffic is essentially non-existent. There are no other cars to get out of the way for, so this infrastructure is wasted money on something that is unnecessary unless North Korea is expecting a major population boom in the next couple of years. Maybe North Korea is thinking about bringing in several million refugees...

The infrastructure sure looks nice, though!

Double-barreled mountain tunnels.

Some More Quick Things About North Korea:

★ *The bus stopped at Koryo Songgyungwan, which is a university originally constructed in 992AD and then rebuilt in 1602.*

★ *Kim showed me the oldest wooden printer and the oldest book in the world from the year 1042. He also showed me the oldest metal printer, also from the 11th century.*

★ *I was talking to Kim about some of the attractive women I had seen in North Korea. He told me, "Women in north beautiful. Man in south is handsome!" Choose your location based on your orientation!*

★ *It is pretty interesting to see army trucks loaded with soldiers and hanging from the rearview mirror is a FIFA soccer ball ornament. That accessory seemed very out of place with the rest of the arrangement.*

★ *Men retire at the age of 60 in North Korea and women at the age of 55.*

★ When President Kim Il-sung visited an area of DPRK called Sariwon, he saw a flower that he thought was beautiful. It was a magnolia, which immediately became the national flower.

★ At one point as we drove down the highway, there were busloads of soldiers out watering plants. The entire side of the hill in the middle of the countryside was covered in soldiers with buckets.

★ Soldiers with flares stand on the highway to mark detours for safety. There are no cars and there is nothing in any direction for miles, and yet there is a soldier charged with making sure cars are safe.

A stop to visit students in an outdoor class. Uniformity.

A FEW MORE PHOTOS
OF THE ROAD:

North Korean landscape.

The road might not look rough in this photo, but believe me...

Many North Koreans out working the fields together as a team.

Thank goodness for that traffic-directing soldier. Without him, chaos may break out at any second.

*If you think that times might be tough in North Korea
right now, it sure looks a lot better than it was.*

Farming with a steel-wheeled tractor in some very saturated conditions.

It is easy to appreciate how the land has been worked so high up the mountains.

North Korea: Prettier than I was expecting!

THE NORTH KOREAN SIDE OF THE DMZ
DAY 2-PART 2

Demilitarized Zone, Kaesong, DPRK

A blurry image of the Korean peninsula featuring the DMZ line.

We arrived at the Korean Demilitarized Zone (DMZ) after a long and rough three-hour journey from Pyongyang. A lot of soldiers were in the vicinity of the DMZ. It was the first time on the trip that we were allowed to freely take photos of the scene even if there were soldiers in the background. My North Korean guide, Kim, had told me earlier that a soldier would be our guide through the DMZ to ensure our safety.

Our bus brought us pretty close to the zone. The Chinese were inside a gift shop buying T-shirts, chocolates, and crazy postcards with anti-American propaganda. Not me—I was standing outside with my guide. I was writing down some information in my notepad that Kim had told me about the Korean DMZ.

> I hadn't thought of my mistake until later—that I was at the Korean DMZ, taking notes. It just did not cross my mind at all...

I was just doing what I normally do...writing down interesting things that people tell me. As I was doing this, a North Korean soldier in uniform and a hat walked towards Kim and me. The soldier asked Kim where I was from. Kim told him that I was from Canada. I realized at that moment what had probably brought on this question, and I subtly slid my notepad into my back pocket. I could see the soldier studying me. His eyes intimidated me as he looked me over and began asking Kim other questions.

> Essentially, the soldier and I had a conversation, but all of the words went through Kim to be translated in each direction as the soldier could not speak English and I could not speak Korean.

I wanted to be warm and shook the hand of the soldier to introduce myself. He squeezed my hand very hard to show me whatever he felt that might show me. I did not like his eyes at all, nor did I like his terrifying plastic smile when he spoke. I felt like I could see through his eyes to episodes in his life where he had pulled the fingernails off of men in order to make them talk about things they did not want to discuss.

This is essentially how the Kim-translated conversation with the soldier went:

North Korean Soldier: *"May I ask you what your occupation is?"*

Me, the journalist: *"I work with oil."*

Soldier: *"Ah, I think that is probably a good job."*

Me, the oilfield man: *"The money is good. The hours are long."*

Soldier: *"Did you know that today, June 25th, 2017, is the 67th anniversary of the war?"*

Me: *"Yes, Kim told me that earlier."*

Soldier: *"Canada, your country, fought with the Americans, against us in the war. What do you have to say about that?"*

Me: (Very uncomfortable laughter) *"Umm, I think I am not going to answer that."*

Soldier: *"So, in Canada, you live in the middle of America. There is America below you and America above you."*

Me: *"Well, that is not quite right. America is below us, and there is Alaska to the northwest of us, but Canada is actually a bigger country in size."*

Soldier: *"Did you know that we killed 440,000 Americans in the war?"*

Me: *"Whoa, I had no idea that was the number."*

Someone called the soldier at that moment and he walked away. It was a huge relief. All I wanted to do was get away from the man. The way he looked at me out of the corner of his eye was too much for me. I could feel his intense hatred towards Americans, and as far as he was concerned that was essentially my nationality as well.

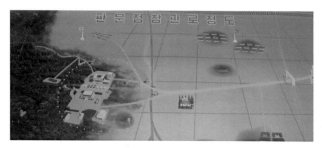

The map on the wall of the Korean DMZ.

As luck would have it, about 10 minutes later, that very same soldier was our guide as we crossed into the DMZ. He told us that they do not have any heavy weapons with them on the north side of the DMZ but that the south has them along their border. The soldier informed us that in North Korea they only carry pistols for protection as they patrol the border.

We then had to line up individually like soldiers to be led through the area to get on buses to get closer to the Korean DMZ.

★ *The DMZ is 250 km long and divides the Korean peninsula roughly in half.*

★ *The DMZ is 4 km wide, as North Korea and South Korea each have 2 km of DMZ space to the line.*

★ *Just north of the DMZ on the North Korean side, there is a farmer's village of 250 people. Years ago when I was in South Korea, I also visited the DMZ from the south side where we could see a place we were told was referred to by the South Koreans as "Propaganda Village." We were informed that it was a beautiful town of empty shells that Kim Jong-il had built so that the South Koreans would look across the border and see the incredible prosperity of North Korea and wish they had the same success. I was unable to locate this village from the north side of the border. All I could see was the small farming village with an apartment complex in the middle of it. Perhaps that is what we were viewing from the south side of the border.*

The soldier took us around the North Korean side of the DMZ and led us into a building that had been constructed just before the end of the war. When the soldier spoke of the war, he talked of how the DPRK had defeated the Americans. I had always thought of the war as North Korea versus South Korea, and communism versus democracy. But, the soldier made it clear that it was a war between Korea and the United States.

We were told that the Americans wanted the Korean peninsula as a mainland that would grant them direct front-line land access to China so they would be able to keep an eye on the Chinese. At that time, Korea was newly independent—after being under Japanese rule since 1910—and had only been free for five years since the end of WWII, so the US thought they would easily be able to take control. However, Korea was not willing to give up and let the Americans in. The soldier said that something similar happened in Vietnam not long after the Korean War for associated reasons, but the Vietnamese also stood their ground.

The soldier went on to explain that the Koreans handed the Americans their first defeat in war history. He used strong words like "embarrassment," "defeat" and "disgrace" when he spoke of the United States. After one year of fighting, he told us that the Americans asked to have a talk because they were being heavily defeated. He said it was a dirty move by the Americans as they used the talk as an excuse to plan another attack. America eventually asked to sign a ceasefire to put an end to their casualties.

The UN flag left behind by the US after the ceasefire agreement.

The Americans wanted to sign the ceasefire agreement in a tent, but Korean President Kim Il-sung had a building constructed where the ceasefire would be signed. He said that he wanted the building in place so that it would be there to remind him of America's embarrassment forever. That was the building we were standing in as the North Korean history of the war was depicted to us. We were told that America was so ashamed that they did not bring their own flag to the meeting. They only brought a UN flag and forgot to take the flag with them again when they left. So, the original UN flag still sits on a desk within the DPRK-erected building.

North Korean soldiers standing on guard in front of the DMZ buildings on the line. The large gray building behind is on the South Korean side of the DMZ.

From that building, we were led to another room that soldiers were guarding. In the room was a desk with a microphone wire across the middle. We were told that the cord for the microphone was actually lying directly across the line of the DMZ. The soldier told us that the room we were in is the only place in the entire DMZ where you can be in both North and South Korea. Beautiful irony abounded as a South Korean-manufactured Samsung air conditioner sat on the north side of the building to keep the place at a cool.

With one hand across the alleged DMZ line between North Korea and South Korea.

71

The soldier explained that there have been over 10,000 meetings in the room with the Americans since the ceasefire in the war, because the Americans keep on breaking regulations previously agreed upon. He said that the North Koreans have asked to change the ceasefire into a peace treaty, but the United States will not agree to the transition. So, the North Koreans only think of the past 64 years as a break in the war.

Wow!

A visit to the North Korean side of the DMZ turned out to be an extremely fascinating experience...

The last signature ever of Kim Il-sung on the day he died.

North Korean soldiers on guard in the DMZ room where the microphone wires along the middle of the desk indicate the exact line between North and South Korea.

North Korean soldier who led our tour through the North Korean side of the DMZ after having an awfully intense conversation with me. Those terrifying eyes will probably haunt me forever.

It is not much of a photo, but this represents what we were told is a farming village on the north side of the DMZ.

*You are probably never going to come across another
postcard quite like that in your life.*

*Young female soldier at the North Korean
DMZ restaurant gift shop.*

BACK TO PYONGYANG
DAY 2–PART 3

Southern DPRK

After the visit to the DMZ, we eventually bounced our way back to Pyongyang, and went into the metro station that we were told is the deepest in the world. The metro system was built from 1968 to 1973 and the 70 stops average 100 meters of depth. The metro was the equivalent of $0.05 to ride.

The Pyongyang Metro system, the deepest in the world.

We rode the metro underground from one station to another. Each station is elaborately different with gorgeous paintings of Kim Il-sung and Kim Jong-il, as well as mosaics, bright colors and fancy chandeliers. Classical music plays through speakers in the entire metro system.

There was a plaque from 1987 inside of one of the metro stations to commemorate the time Kim Il-sung and Kim Jong-il visited that particular station at that particular time. Allegedly, it was a glorious moment for that station.

This beautiful metro station in Pyongyang looks more like an opera house.

From the metro we were bused to the original home of Kim Il-sung. It was pouring rain and tough to want to explore, but we put bags on our feet and doubled up under a few umbrellas. Kim Il-sung's parents were keepers of a graveyard, but all of the graves have been moved today so that the house sits alone in the forest.

A Quick and Vague North Korean Timeline Featuring Kim Il-sung:

★   *Korea was under Japanese colonial rule from 1910-1945.*

★   *Kim Il-sung was born in 1912.*

★ In 1925, at the age of 13, Kim Il-sung went off to fight in the war against Japan to liberate Korea. His entire family went with him to fight (his father, mother, brother, uncle and cousin).

★ After a 20-year battle, Kim Il-sung, was the only surviving member of his family, and in 1945 he liberated Korea.

★ Kim Il-sung went on to dictate in the DPRK for the next 49 years until his death in 1994.

> And now you know a little more about the last 100-plus years in North Korean history!
>
> Do not worry. It was all new to me, as well.

Thirteen-year-old Kim Il-sung heading off to war to eventually liberate Korea from the Japanese.

We went for dinner and Wu Zheng Yu ended up sitting at my table again. So, it was a similar scenario to the night before as I made Wu Zheng Yu keep up and drink a lot of beer with me. The poor guy... he seemed to be biting off more than he could chew.

Dinner was a lot of fun. I talked a lot of nonsense with the Chinese to the point where one older man told me, "I love you!" and another told me in broken English that his wife was going to find a nice Chinese girl for me. That sounded like a pretty good idea...

*Karaoke taking place in our restaurant. I really enjoyed
the lyrics to this missile-launching video.*

Back at the hotel, I met up with Jo, the Chinese girl I was hanging around with the night before, and we explored the Yanggakdo International Hotel. I am sure there were no more than 50 people staying in the entire 47-story building, but what a place it would be if it was full.

Hanging out on the marble staircase of the hotel.

There is an area downstairs in the hotel where there is a swimming pool with a bar. There is a ping-pong table with a bar. A billiards bar. A karaoke room. A massage room. The North Korean women running all of these areas of the hotel were so sweet. I asked to get a photo with the ping-pong room lady. She shook her head to tell me no, but then nodded yes and said, "Play ping-pong..." It was unbelievably cute. There was also a bowling alley downstairs. Jo had never been bowling before, so we went there to give it a try. That turned out to be a lot of fun.

Kim showed up at the bowling alley in the hotel to find me, as I guess he thought we had been apart for too long. Kim also tried his hand at bowling for the first time, which ended in a gutter ball, but he seemed to really enjoy his one throw as he was glowing with pleasure after.

This is how I asked our bowling waitress if she was married. She laughed and nodded, which seemed to explain that she is.

At the end of the night, Jo and I were sitting at the bowling alley bar, drinking water and talking while communicating through picture-drawing with the North Korean girl running the space. We had a lot of laughs and Jo and I were quite touchy. But, when we took the elevator to head back to our rooms, she said she was tired and was going to sleep. I made an alternative suggestion about how we could hang out in my room together, which was certainly a far better idea than not hanging out in my room together, but she must have felt an obligation to the elevator floor-botton she had already pushed. Typical scared and shy Chinese. We could have had a 40th-floor hotel room blast...

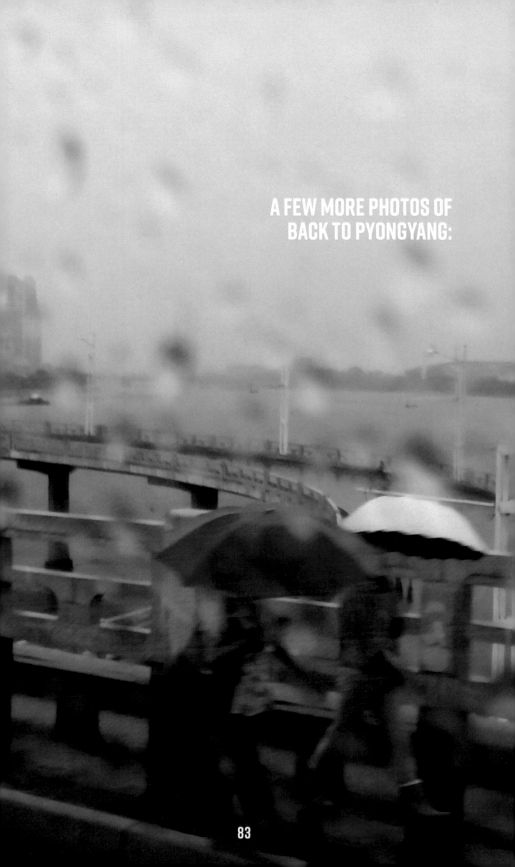

A FEW MORE PHOTOS OF
BACK TO PYONGYANG:

The Monument to the Three Charters for National Reunification.
The highway travels through this massive structure.

A photo that really shows the mood of the moment.

Heading down into the deepest metro system in the world in Pyongyang.

In the Pyongyang Metro. A giant mural of Kim Il-sung making North Koreans happy.

Kim Il-sung and Kim Jong-il, always riding the metro with you...

Giant metro mural of Kim Jong-il.

The metro of Pyongyang is art.

KUMGANG, NORTH KOREA
DAY 3

Pyongyang, DPRK

Kim, my North Korean guide, could not wait to see me in the morning to ask what happened with Jo, the Chinese girl, last night. Nothing happened, but I enjoyed his nosiness so much that I remained silent and decided not to tell him anything...

"Good morning, Pyongyang!"

After breakfast at the Yanggakdo International Hotel, we loaded onto a bus and headed for Mt. Kumgang, which is in the south-east corner of the DPRK, right next to the South Korean border.

I was told that Mt. Kumgang is the most beautiful mountain in the entire Korean peninsula. According to my itinerary, "It is a world-wide celebrated mountain." I had never known anyone to celebrate it and I have a lot of international friends, but I was excited to see it!

The road from Pyongyang.

Some Quick Korean Numbers:

★ *The Korean peninsula = 223,000 km2*

★ *DPRK (North Korea) = 120,000 km2*

★ *The population of Korea = 80 million*

★ *The population of DPRK = 20 million*

Buckle up and hang on. This is going to happen way faster than it should.

Had I known that the trip was going to be an eight-hour drive across the country to get to Mt. Kumgang on even rougher roads than the ones we took to the DMZ yesterday, I would have taken a pass and asked for an altered itinerary. If you are in the mood for a bus ride where you wear your seat belt, not for safety, but because you are tired of being bounced off and out of your seat, then this is the trip for you.

> It felt like I was a patient in a psych ward who
> had to be tied down.

At the same time, a North Korean girl was on the microphone nearly yelling in Chinese about South and North Korean relations for three hours of the journey. A psych ward may have been a more serene option because those three hours of her on the microphone while I was being tossed around in my seat nearly pushed me over the edge. I was not a happy traveler. I could not help my mood. It really fell apart. An hour into the trip, I realized I had seven more to go and wished the drive would end already. It would be eight hours back again tomorrow. I still had 15 more hours of a road trying to shake the fillings out of my teeth...

Sometimes it is not easy to smile. A 16-hour round-trip road trip on a bus from Pyongyang to Mt. Kumgang, North Korea, is one of those times.

The Monument to the Three Charters for National Reunification.

Along the way, we stopped at the Monument to the Three Charters for National Reunification to take photos. I was standing in the middle of the road on the empty highway to get the perfect snapshot. My guide, Kim, gave me heck for being on the road and told me what I was doing was dangerous. There was not even the sound of a car coming on the horizon... It really made me think about how interesting it would be to bring Kim somewhere like Bangkok or Rio de Janeiro where six lanes of traffic squeeze into four lanes, and somehow you have to figure out how to cross that street by foot. Just the look in his eyes at that moment would be something to see!

A beautiful spot in a North Korean village called Yangdok.

There is no Internet in North Korea, but Kim had a smartphone. The phone was a brand called "Pyongyang," which he told me is the biggest phone company in the DPRK. On his phone, Kim could browse something called "Intronet." The server is DPRK-regulated and allows North Koreans to see what the government wants them to see. Kim was reading out the news headlines he translated for me:

"3.4 Million Nigerians Have Aids."

"Ukraine Is a Mess."

"Millions of People in Peru Have No Water."

"Trump Overrules Agreement with Cuba."

"Antarctica Is Melting."

It seems safer to just stay in the DPRK and be taken care of with all of the madness out there in the world... When I asked him about it, Kim told me that he thinks the media in North Korea is good.

With Intronet, Kim is able to look at maps, but only maps of North Korea. As well, he could use his phone to listen to different types of local music (including North Korean rock!), and he could use something similar to Facetime to see and speak with his friends. There is no such thing as an email address and there is no access to media outlets other than the ones the government provides. There are five television channels in North Korea, and Kim is also able to watch any programs from any of these channels on his phone.

Locals off from work who had been fishing in the river at a town called Wonsan.

Of the males that I would regularly see in the DPRK as we traveled through the countryside, it seemed most were either soldiers or farmers. Some of the soldiers' faces were very young. The oldest faces were those of farmers who were bent over when they walked to the point that their backs were nearly horizontal and they required walking sticks. Planting and harvesting by hand for a lifetime appears to be very hard on a body. Kim told me that office workers have work schedules of six days on and one day off, whereas farmers have a schedule of ten days on and one day off.

Even on a lousy day, the North Korean coastline looks pretty.

Some More Interesting Things About North Korea:

★ *As we traveled east toward the coast for four hours, we passed trucks here and there, broken down with their hoods opened, smoke billowing out, and usually a North Korean man would be lying underneath the vehicle with oily truck parts surrounding him on the ground.*

★ *At one point we slowly passed a three-ton truck that was stopped in the middle of the road. In the back of the truck was a load of passengers: farmers, soldiers, and well-dressed women heading somewhere. The truck had a crank start, just as engines had in North America before the 1950s. Two soldiers were taking turns cranking the handle of the truck in an attempt to get the engine started. I wanted a photo of the scene, but it was not allowed because the men cranking the truck were in uniform.*

★ *Military service in DPRK is not compulsory, but much of the population enlists because they are proud to serve their country.*

★ Kim estimated that the average age for males to marry is 28, and females around 26.

★ There are no horses in North Korea, anywhere. Oxen are everywhere pulling wooden carts down dirt paths and one-bottom wooden plows through the earth, but there are no horses.

★ I asked Kim if there is any crime in DPRK. He told me that it doesn't really exist. He said there is a slight possibility of a North Korean pickpocketing another, but that is the rare extent of crime. I asked him if anyone would ever steal a bike. He said it would NEVER happen.

★ Oftentimes, highways tunnel directly through mountains rather than around them. Some of the tunnels are as long as three kilometers. Outside of every tunnel, a stand is erected where a soldier is posted to pay attention to the traffic. As well, there is a soldier at the other end of the tunnel, doing the same thing for the vehicles traveling in the opposite direction.

★ The east-west road from Pyongyang to Wonsan was four lanes wide, and our bus used all four lanes in one direction to try to utilize the smoothest parts.

★ In Wonsan, the city where we would turn to drive south, we stopped for lunch and ate snakehead fish (a scary-looking fish that probably matches the imagery currently in your mind). On the street after, as I went to take a photo, I heard two little voices behind me. When I turned around, two little North Korean girls of about seven years of age saw my face, shrieked, and ran away! It was very cute.

★ It is bad luck to pour your own beer in North Korea.

★ Sometimes meals in North Korea require a cigarette break.

★ Our bus driver had a special pair of driving gloves that he would always put on before he would take the wheel once we boarded his vessel.

★   *The front seat of the bus is the best place to sit because it offers a forward view in addition to the sides. Oftentimes, it was uncomfortable to be sitting there because every couple of kilometers on the highway, in the middle of nowhere, a soldier is stationed. Nearly every one of those soldiers would see me and would follow me with his eyes until we passed.*

In a store at a rest area on the way to Mt. Kumgang, I purchased a bottle of Bem Sul, which translates to "Snake Liquor." The Bem Sul bottle cost me $7.80. It is 60% alcohol, and there is a snake inside of the bottle. I was not sure if I would be able to bring it back into my country, but it was worth a $7.80 try. At times on the drive from Pyongyang to Mt. Kumgang, I wondered if I should just drink it to combat my ill feelings due to the rough road and the yelling in Chinese.

Bem Sul.

Snake liquor.

Eventually, eight (non) short hours later, we arrived at our destination in the Kuryongyon District and headed to Lagoon Samil. The lagoon is known as one of the "Eight Scenic Wonders of East Korea." I love how places in North Korea have dramatic lists for pocket areas. Lagoon Samil is famous for its beauty and a legend that comes with it: an emperor once visited the lagoon with intentions of taking a rest there for a day. Enthralled by the beauty of the lagoon, he ended up staying for three days.

Lagoon Samil translates to "Lagoon Three" which is in reference to the emperor's three-day stay.

Lagoon Samil, aka Three-Day Stay.

Our hotel and dinner was in Kumgang, North Korea, a town that was built up by Hyundai and the South Koreans in 2002, when the relationship between North and South Korea was better. For five years, South Koreans were allowed to visit North Korea to see Mt. Kumgang and have the opportunity to see separated family members. In 2007, relations between the two nations soured again, South Korea was kicked out, and the town of Kumgang essentially became abandoned.

As a result of the South Korean banning, Kumgang is a beautiful ghost town only frequented by Chinese tourists and occasional North Koreans on holiday (who stay in the elaborate hotels for approximately $20/night). There is a giant concert hall that is empty, a discarded bank, closed-down restaurants, a deserted duty-free store, and only two of the five hotels in the village are still operational. The Oekumgang Hotel we were staying in had no more than 20 guests in the 10-story building.

Kumgang, North Korea.

Oh, hey 2000 won North Korean note. You look familiar!

As we were checked in, I asked for a pre-arranged wake-up call and was told that the phones were not working. Apparently, the South Koreans set up the phone system in the hotel, and when they were expelled from the country, they removed whatever access was needed to run the hotel telephones.

Abandoned in North Korea. The Koreans love top-floor revolving restaurants.

For dinner, we went as a group to a restaurant. The Chinese finished their meal early and went back to the hotel with their guide, but Kim was still eating so I stayed with him. He told me that I was not allowed to walk the 200 meters back to the hotel alone as a foreigner because of the danger of the outbreak of war. It is surely a control tactic by the government, but imagine being North Korean and living your entire life thinking that a war might break out at any given moment...

At Kumgang, another depiction of 13-year-old Kim Il-sung heading off to war.

Back at the hotel I went to the gift shop and had a great time teaching the cute North Korean employee how to high-five. She had never done it before and it was really sweet to watch her try to get it down. I kept on returning to the shop to smile at her and high-five her as it would make her giggle so much. The innocence in locals is quite a treat to come across. They may be the most innocent civilians I have ever met in my life.

I brought a bag of Chinese candy with me, but it was difficult to give sweets away as the North Koreans are too polite to allow themselves to take gifts. So, I would let them watch me leave pieces of candy on desks and tables for them to collect later. When I would return a few moments later, the candies would always be gone.

I found this image at our restaurant. Why it was there, I do not know, but it is pretty freaking amazing!

In the evening, I took Kim for a beer in our hotel bar, but gave him my Chinese money (it is illegal for foreigners to have local North Korean currency) to pay for our drinks. I suggested that with him paying, he could probably get a better price than I would. This tactic initially confused him. He must have known the "foreigner" beer price because he nearly peed in his pants with delight when the bartender told him the low price that he had to pay for our beer, and then the price was lowered again for him because he is a tour guide. He loved it and said to me, beaming, "I think you are a much more clever man than me!"

Kim will remember that move for the rest of his life.

An empty and abandoned concert hall in Kumgang.

At the bar, Kim and I were talking about different Korean women in the vicinity. We were discussing which girls he thought were pretty and which ones I thought were pretty. We had very different opinions. I asked him if he had many female admirers. He told me that a man who women desire in North Korea is a man who has: a) done military service, b) supports the Workers' Party of Korea, and c) has studied at university.

Kim reiterated, "Girls like it more if a man has done military service. It is an honor to do it, and I have not done mine yet. They think that if you have not done military service, you're not a man. You're a boy."

A FEW MORE PHOTOS OF KUMGANG, NORTH KOREA:

*This is a view from my 40th-floor hotel room on the island where we
stayed in the Yanggakdo International Hotel in Pyongyang*

A beautifully dilapidated stadium just behind the Yanggakdo International Hotel.

The Tomb of King Tongmyong (58-19 BCE).

Asians gates are fascinating. They always have an amazing and unique style in each distinct culture.

Meet Kokuryo, an emperor who was a crack shot with a bow and arrow at the age of one. That sounds quite biblical.

Friends, I do not make a lot of demands, but when I go, if no one makes a painting of me riding through the clouds on a golden chariot drawn by dragons, it will seem like a life wasted!

North Korean flag-bearing highway mountain tunnel.

That time in North Korea when I went into the restaurant bathroom to wash my hands but there was a bucket of small fish in the way.

It was when I was taking this photo that I heard the little voices behind me and turned around to see two little girls who made eye contact with me, shrieked, and then ran away. It was my favorite moment of the day.

A road that can really take it out of you after eight hours bouncing across it on a bus. This is was an attempt to take a level photo.

Pretty Lagoon Samil.

I have a hard time comprehending the amount of work that went into carving these words into these giant stones. There was a date beside the writing on another stone just like this one. It was made to seem as if all the writing was done in one day. That must have been a very long day.

Ladies passing by on bikes.

The nearly vacant Oekumgang Hotel in Kumgang.

Kumgang is a beautiful little town.

Abandoned duty-free store in Kumgang.

An empty bank in a sad little town that was once a buzzing little haven during the limited North and South Korean partial-visitation reunification from 2002-2007.

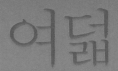

LIFE IN THE DPRK
DAY 4-PART I

Kumgang, DPRK

The doorbell to my hotel room in Kumgang, North Korea, went off at 06:00. The front desk sent someone to my room to wake me up because the telephones in the hotel did not work.

Breakfast.
Bus.
Back on the road.

My group of seven Chinese tourists and I were off to Mt. Kumgang...

This is what North Korea looks like. Who would have known?

North Korea is really beautiful. One would never think of North Korea as a gorgeous place because the general masses are more likely to think of war and nuclear missiles when the country comes up in conversation. However, the DPRK is green and lush. The ocean side is a vibrant blue and the mountains are wonderful. The pretty nature seems so misplaced and totally contrasts preconceived mental notions of how the land may look. Green, North Korea? What?

Along the road, soldiers are stationed every couple of kilometers, keeping everything in check. They hardly ever acknowledged our bus, but on occasions when they did, they saluted us as we passed. Checkpoints are frequent, but it was rare that Kim had to get off the bus and show the soldiers his credentials.

A pretty waterfall on the North Korean mountainside.

North Korea has been in a constant state of war, either physically or mentally, from 1910 until today. Life in the northern part of the Korean peninsula has consisted of over 100 years of battle. In 1910, the Japanese colonized Korea and Koreans spent the next thirty-five years fighting until they were eventually freed in 1945. There were five years of peace and then the Korean War began in 1950 and carried through until 1953.

There has been a ceasefire since 1953, but there is a constant threat of war and the DPRK is always mentally prepared for it to break out again. These conditions are normal to the North Koreans, so they don't know any different, but it must be tough on them.

Regardless of Kim's ideology of, 'Women in north beautiful. Man in south is handsome,' I find the women in South Korea to be more attractive than the North Koreans. I wonder if that has to do with the mental stress in North Korea that eventually shows up physically...

Taking a photo of Kim in my sunglasses to show him how cool he looks! When the sun came out and I put on my shades for the day, Kim laughed at me and said, "Very strange!" He had never seen anything like them before. When I made him try them on it made him giggle!

Life in North Korea means that Kim, and every other North Korean, wears one of two red pins. One of the pins has the images of Kim Il-sung and Kim Jong-il on it, and the other just has Kim Jong-il. Every single North Korean wears the pin as a part of their identity. Everyone. I asked Kim if he has extras at home, which he confirmed. I asked him if it would be okay for me to have one of his pins. He told me that it would be impossible for me to get one.

I offered Kim my sunglasses for one of his pins.
No chance.
I offered him my belt that he liked.
Nope.

Kim told me, "I cannot trade. We North Koreans wear the pin over our hearts, because that is where President Kim Il-sung and Chairman Kim Jong-il live." I was not even allowed to take a photo of the pin. They truly love their Great

Leader (Kim Il-sung) and their Dear Leader (Kim Jong-il) with devotion. I have never seen people who are so passionate about their heads of state anywhere else in the world. I asked him about Marshal Kim Jong-un, and how North Koreans feel about him. He said that the country loves their newest leader.

A lovely little DPRK waterfall.

Kim and I left the Chinese tourists behind on our 90-minute hike up Mt. Kumgang. Age worked in our favor. It was a very beautiful trek and there was no one else on the mountain. We watched the waterfall at the top for some time and hiked back down to wait for the Chinese to reach the top and return to the bottom. In the meantime, Kim and I drank beer while we waited.

When I paid for the beer with Chinese currency, I was given back some change in Chinese yuan, but when they did not have enough yuan they gave me back a US $5 note. I found it pretty bizarre to be given American money in North Korea. I also found it peculiar to get change back in different currencies at once. Trying to double-check the accuracy of your change is pretty tricky when you are dealing with three currencies, two of which are supposed to make up for the combined change together of the original price in a currency that you are not even allowed to handle as a foreigner. I found it easier to assume that the North Koreans were not cheaters. The locals seem to have little use for money in their government system anyhow...

North Koreans looking at my sticker with a beaver image. It turns out that the word for "Beaver" in Korean is phonetically "Hae ri so." My last name is Harris and I have been called Harriso in a Korean accent before when my name has been mispronounced. That is an amazing coincidence! The Koreans have accidentally been calling me Beaver for years.

There were two North Korean waitresses taking care of customers where Kim and I sat outside. At the table next to us were a couple of North Korean men in their thirties, eating and drinking beer. I could see both of the waitresses looking at me, but only one of them was brave enough to come and interact with me. We had a small conversation in English and she asked my nationality and my age. After building up her courage, the other waitress came to look at me and say hello. I shook her hand and introduced myself, and then she ran away giggling. It was really sweet.

Kim said to me, "I think you like chat with girls!" I told Kim that I really liked him, but that I was hoping to trade him for three North Korean girls. It made him laugh. When the Chinese finally got back from the mountain and we went to leave our table, the shy waitress said to me, "See... see... see you again!" and let me take a photo with her. Her willingness to be in a photo came as a quite a surprise!

Sweet and shy.

Some Things About North Korean:

★ *In the Mt. Kumgang area, there was a giant carving in stone with three-meter-tall characters which Kim translated to me as reading, "Bright star of Juche, Kim Jong-il." If you remember from earlier, Juche is defined as, 'The capacity to shape our destiny.'"*

★ *The roads are empty through the countryside when driving in North Korea, but as we got closer to the cities and towns, the roads would begin to get busy—never with cars, but with bicycles, people walking, and oxen pulling carts around.*

★ *In Wonsan, when we stopped for lunch again on the way back to Pyongyang, I discovered that the town had a set of the massive bronze statues of Kim Il-sung and Kim Jong-il that I had seen in so many photos. I had Kim walk with me to take a photo of them, but we had to respectfully keep a distance from the statues. Behind the massive bronze figures was a giant building with a gorgeous mural painted on its side. I asked Kim about the building. He told me that it was the Revolutionary Museum of Korea, but that foreigners are not allowed inside. Wow, it would have been fascinating to get inside of that building. A decree of non-admittance certainly raises human curiosity!*

A FEW MORE PHOTOS
OF LIFE IN THE DPRK:

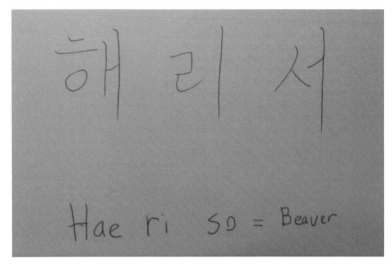

Hae ri so = Beaver

That is a fun bit of Korean information to get when your nickname is Beaver and your family name is Harris...

One difference between North Korea and the rest of the world—there would be hordes of locals and tourists in water that looked like this anywhere else on the planet.

*Another marker indicating that Kim Il-sung graced this spot with his presence
at some point in his life. The date of such a major event is always marked.*

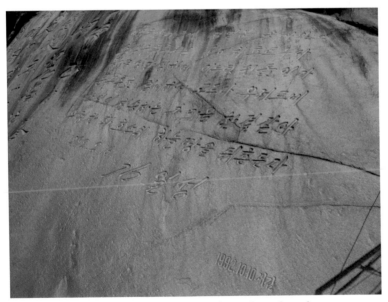

Words of wisdom by Kim Jong-il carved into the rock.

This is where Kim and I were drinking beer at the bottom of the mountain. I am not at all sure what is going on here, but we have some type of frog band.

A nice little stream in a country known for nuclear weapons.
Each aspect is such a contrast to the other.

Those are Korean characters carved into the rocks, but Kim said the characters are in ancient Korean and he was unable to read what they say.

Our North Korean bus driver. He would not turn the wheel until he had his professional driving gloves on.

Locals having lunch on the side of the road under the shade of a tree.

When you meet vehicles on the road, they are either military vehicles or farming trucks. The farming trucks are always very old and tired.

I know. Just look at that blue...in North Korea.

A little place to escape the sun for the farmers working the fields.

Carts on the side of the road while the oxen are grazing in the field, having lunch.

A bicycle doubling as a wheelbarrow. That is a bike-load of cooking fuel!

Rubber-tired oxen carts for use in the city, as opposed to the wooden-wheeled carts used in the countryside.

Life as it looks on the coast of the DPRK.

A country village for the farmers of the region.

The crossing arm is a wooden pole painted to look like the crossing arms of the western world. I assume with confidence that it has never happened in the history of North Korea that a driver fell asleep at the wheel. There is not enough time to relax while driving to be able to catch accidental winks.

The empty south-eastern coastline of North Korea.

Local fisherman trying his luck in a pond at the side of a rice paddy.

North Korean clams seem to stick their tongues out when they have been conquered. Attitude clams!

Giant bronze statues of Kim Il-sung and Kim Jong-il.

A RETURN TO THE CAPITAL
DAY 4-PART 2

On the road to Pyongyang, DPRK

As we were making our way back to the North Korean capital city of Pyongyang, I asked Kim about jobs in his country. He told me that all jobs pay nearly the same. A dentist makes a similar amount of money to a bus driver. I wanted to know how it worked, and he told me that you can do whatever you want to do in the DPRK as long as you study and educate yourself. As an example, I asked him if it would be possible to run a hydro-power station. He said you would just have to study for it in university, and once you completed your course, the government would find you a job.

Something is getting done around here.

Kim said that getting into the workforce through education is the same in North Korea as it is in western countries, with the difference being that westerners then have to compete for jobs once they are finished their studies. In the DPRK, the government gives people their place of work once they finish their education.

I asked him about courses filling up and there not being enough jobs for the people finishing their studies. He told me he could not think of a case where there were more people looking for jobs than there were jobs. Kim said if he wanted to be a doctor, he could study hard to become a doctor.

I love this old tractor and the stack of hay. The entire country participates in the planting and harvesting of crops.

The DPRK is set up so that all citizens have to do some mandatory farming. No matter what your job is in the country, you will have to do some farm work. Kim said that he has to do 10 days of planting and 10 days of harvest ever year. He goes to the same farm where 10 people meet to work, and it is always the same people that he works with on the farm.

Working the land.

I asked Kim if he enjoys the farming. He said he prefers the harvest, as it is not as hard on the back, but that he enjoys both seasons as it is such a social event and he gets to spend time with those same 10 people twice a year. Every person in North Korea does mandatory farm work. The system is pretty great for Kim, as it is a break from his normal life.

Earlier, when we were traveling through the countryside and passed through a village, I noticed a sign and asked Kim to translate the words. It was the image of a farmer and said in Korean, "Let Us Help Farming!" Everyone seems to be behind the idea.

Evening entertainment with dinner.

When we arrived back in Pyongyang and headed to the Yanggakdo International Hotel after dinner, it was around 21:00. A couple of days earlier, I had been pressuring Kim to take me to a bar where the workers go in Pyongyang, but that night was the anniversary of the war and no places were open. So, again I tried to convince Kim to take me out after we had settled back into the hotel. Kim was tired and told me that it would be best to go to bed. However, it was my last night of seeing anything in Pyongyang that was not part of a tour...

The background scene for a karaoke song in a local restaurant.

I wanted to see the city at night and I really wanted a break from the organized tourism. I wanted a small piece of my own version of Pyongyang, North Korea.

Kim did not want to go out, but I cranked up the pressure and guilt-tripped him about the torture I had been forced to endure on the tour bus the past two days, and how I really did not want to go back to the double room that, for the first time, I was going to have to share with one of the Chinese tourists. I felt bad about the guilt trip, but I had to be selfish because it was my only chance to see the city. I knew that Kim wanted nothing more than for me to go to bed, but after a 90-second intensive and convincing rant, he caved and agreed to take me out.

Hurray!
Well, a guilty hurray...

The problem was that I would have to hire a driver to take us around and I would need to take another guide with us because there always had to be two guides with foreigners. I had Kim, and the Chinese had their microphone-yeller, but we were always together...

Kim made a few phone calls and then spoke to another guide. The other guide told Kim that there was a Mexican in the hostel who would probably want to go out, as well. That sounded fine to me, so the other guide went to find a man my age named Juan Carlos (how Mexican!), and the four of us got into the car with a driver who took us to a bar.

*Our own very bright bar in Pyongyang, opened just
for us because it was after 20:00.*

The establishment was completely empty except for the four of us and our driver when we entered. Juan Carlos and I ordered a juice for the driver, a round of beer for everyone else, and a bottle of soju—Korean liquor that quickly reminded my brain to make my mouth slur every time I talked after taking the initial shot. That was at about 22:00. I would later find out that when Kim was on the phone earlier at the hotel, he was calling bars and had to convince a manager to open one up for us. The manager then had to get some girls to come in to serve us, as all bars in Pyongyang close at 20:00. Oh... The intensive and convincing guilt from earlier had changed personnel. I ended up wearing that weight...

I knew the nightlife would be quiet in North Korea, but I had no idea it would not even exist after 8 p.m.

When we left the bar after a short visit, I had Kim ask the driver to take us to the Ryugyong Hotel, the 105-story, 330-meter pyramid-shaped unfinished building in Pyongyang commonly seen in photos. Construction on the hotel began in 1987, but North Korea ran out of money and it is still not completed to this day.

At the time construction began on the building, it would have been the tallest hotel in the world. The exterior of the building has since been completed, but the rest of the superstructure remains unfinished. Today, it holds the noble title of the Tallest Unoccupied Building In The World. It was too dark to get a proper photo of the Ryugyong Hotel, but a gorgeous silhouette of it loomed above us from where we stood. When we got into the car to return to our hotel, Kim looked at me and asked, "Are you happy now?" Yes, yes, I was...

We headed back to the Yanggakdo International Hotel to go to bed as I had originally been expected to do a couple of hours before. When I knocked on the door of my room, the older Chinese man with whom I was sharing my room let me in. He seemed to have been waiting up for me. And since it did not appear that I had missed curfew, he hardly seemed grumpy at all.

I hoped he did not snore. I had not consumed nearly enough beer to drown out a snorer...

**A FEW MORE PHOTOS OF
A RETURN TO THE CAPITAL:**

Workers, usually women, pulling weeds from the cracks on the highway.

A local farmer having a rest and admiring his hard work.

A very busy field in the countryside.

The sign in the background says, "Let Us Help Farming."

*Euros... Yuan... When you receive change while traveling in
North Korea, you never know what you are going to get.*

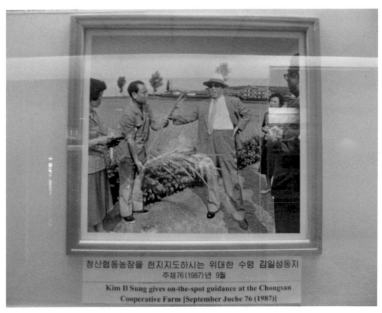

*I wish this photo was clearer, but it is the best I could do in the moment.
I love the description that Kim Il-sung offers "on-the-spot guidance" to
the farmers. Kim Il-sung seemed to have no heroic limitations...*

A crosswalk in Pyongyang, North Korea.

Pyongyang central train station.

EXITING NORTH KOREA
DAY 5

Pyongyang, DPRK

I awoke in the morning to realize that my Chinese roommate was not a snorer! How fortunate!

I was in the shower in my room at the Yanggakdo International Hotel when the telephone rang. I quickly answered the phone in the bathroom with one step from the shower. It was a a wake-up call from Kim and from the other end he said, "Meester Beavers," as he has taken to calling me lately. "It is time to get up." I realized at that moment how strange it has become to answer a proper telephone. That thought is not just because I was answering a telephone mounted next to the toilet in my hotel bathroom... Yes, that scenario is totally bizarre, but a wall connected telephone is nearly history in the western world. A new and modern scale to know that you are in a faraway place is the frequency in which you find yourself answering a landline rather than a cellular phone...

Colorful Pyongyang.

The wake-up call had come earlier than I expected. Kim told me it was because we were leaving North Korea today and the hotel staff needed to come and inspect the room to make sure there was nothing broken or missing before we moved out. I had only been in the room for a few hours a night to catch a few winks and to shower. There had not been enough time to break anything at the hotel.

North Korea Notes:

★ *The Korean War is referred to as "The Fatherland Liberation War" in North Korea.*

★ *Korea used to be spelled Corea before the Japanese moved in and changed the spelling from a "C" to a "K"' because they did not want Corea to be ahead of Japan in the Roman alphabet.*

★ *Kim said that conditions in North Korea have improved since he was a child. He told me that the life standards are better now, though he was not sure of the exact reason. He guessed some of it was attributed to North Korean coal exportation to China.*

★ *I asked Kim about work and he told me that with free housing, free healthcare, free dental, free beer, free rice, free cloth, free eggs and free meat, he is able to save some of his salary every month in a bank account. I asked him what he does with the money. He said that he saves it for occasions like birthday parties, so he can pay for a big celebration.*

★ *North Korean weddings often take place in a restaurant.*

The tour group checked out and we got on the bus to have one last look around Pyongyang before boarding our train for China at 10:10. We were taken to the Arch of Triumph, which stands overtop of a road in Pyongyang and is 11 meters taller than the Arc de Triomphe in Paris. The North Korean Arch was built in 1982 by President Kim Il-sung to commemorate his 70th birthday. Lining the inside of the arch are 70 sculptures of magnolias as the magnolia was the favorite flower of Kim Il-sung which immediately made it the national flower of the DPRK. Inscribed along the top of the arch are the words to the "Song of General Kim Il-sung."

Arch of Triumph in Pyongyang, North Korea. The "1925" and "1945" in gold represent the number of years Kim Il-sung fought to liberate Korea.

What a birthday... Can you imagine the conversation he must have had in his head as he was shaving on the morning when he got the idea to for the arch? "Yes, that's it! As a gift to my people for my 70ᵗʰ birthday, I will construct a huge arch across a road in honor of myself, and on the top of it I will have the words of my own song written! That is such a good idea! I am Kim Il-sung and I am a genius!"

> It is pretty amazing to think that someone would indulge in themselves so much.

"Happy birthday to me, Kim Il-sung!"

The main square of Pyongyang, just outside of the train station.

I asked Kim about the tombs of Eternal President Kim Il-sung and Chairman Kim Jong-il. He told me that they are both lying in state.

What?

Yes, it is true. Kim Il-sung is on display in a building in one room and Kim Jong-il is in another. Kim told me that he has seen the bodies, and that it is considered an honor to view them. He said the bodies can be visited on special occasions: the birthday of Kim Il-sung, the birthday of Kim Jong-il, the DPRK founding day, and the founding day of the Workers' Party. I asked Kim how they look. He said that both bodies look normal, just as they did in their everyday lives. He told me that they are both wearing the usual clothes that they ordinarily wore.

Wow.

A patriotic roundabout, just across the road from Pyongyang Station.

We were taken to the train station so that we could catch our train back across the country and into China. Outside of the station were some cars driving around. Kim told me that it is the busiest street in North Korea. I told him that the same street would be considered a quiet one in Beijing. His expression showed me that he found that to be peculiar.

*Look at that bus! I cannot even venture a guess to what
year that gorgeous machine was made.*

I still had some money in my pocket, so before leaving Pyongyang and exiting
North Korea, I bought a bottle of North Korean soju and a carton of cigarettes to
give away to my friends. I thought that, as a smoker, it would probably be pretty
cool to have a package of North Korean cigarettes. So, the only souvenirs I picked
up in North Korea were a carton of cigarettes, a bottle of soju, and a bottle of
crazy liquor with a snake inside of it. I guess it says a lot about the lifestyle I have
been leading ...

In the waiting lounge (for foreigners only) of the train
station, there were photos of missiles being launched.
North Koreans are proud to talk about their nuclear
weapons. A North Korean-initiated discussion about
nuclear weapons came up a couple of times during
the trip, though it was difficult to know if the guides
brought it up because they liked to talk about it, or
because they know that foreigners love to ask about the
whole nuclear weapon situation. It is all pretty in-your-
face and they are not trying to hide anything.

*Pyongyang Station. Atop the station are the images of the Great
Leader (Kim Il-sung) and the Dear Leader (Kim Jong-il).*

While we were waiting, I gave Kim 300 Chinese yuan as a tip. I had been told by
the manager of Explore North Korea Tours before I left that if I gave him 100, it
would be a lot. As it turns out, 300 yuan is only $44. And for the information
that Kim gave me, and for the fact that he just spent five days by my side, $44
was a pretty good deal. I actually felt cheap even though I had overtipped by
300%. He was very grateful, though I am not sure what he will use the money
for as he does not have to pay bills, pay for beer, pay for food or pay for housing.
Later, I would find out that a guide's salary for a month is about 500 yuan ($74),
so I gave him more than half a month's pay for five days of work.

Perhaps that makes Kim one of the richest people he knows right now. Imagine
the birthday party he will be able to throw! It could be outrageous—maybe even
in a restaurant!

I gave Kim a hug to say goodbye just before I got on the train as I knew that would
make him very uncomfortable, and it did. That human contact was awful for him!
He was an excellent guide and he turned into a good friend.

Exiting North Korea from the Pyongyang Station platform.

Once again, I was the only white person on the train as it transported us on the journey to China. I was thinking about the trip and about the lives of the North Koreans. Maybe they have it better than us in some ways. They do not have to worry about stress from their jobs. They do not have to worry about money. They do not have to worry about paying rent. They are oblivious to most of the fearmongering media we are force-fed in the rest of the world. I never saw any starving people in North Korea. I never saw any homeless. I was told that kids are free to get themselves to school and to piano lessons as the creeps that parents have to worry about in the rest of the world are not an issue in North Korea.

The people of the DPRK do not have the same everyday stresses that nearly everyone else seems to have. There is, however, the constant threat of war looming in the background of day to day living. I would not trade my life for theirs, but their life was nothing like I expected it to be, and for that you can take your "Oh, but propaganda" arguments and shove it.

> The world is full of inexperienced experts in everything and laptop Mother Teresas.

Everyone who watches common news seems to have an opinion about North Korea and everyone seems to think they know more and can tell me more than I might ever know after having experienced it for myself.

> Of course there was propaganda! But, I came to see the country the way they wanted to present it to me. And, I got a stronger insight to the propaganda machine we are part of in the western part of the world.

It is certain that I was intentionally shown and not shown much about North Korea, but there is only so much that can be totally hidden from your view and only so much that can be shown in a presentation. In North Korea I saw some of the most honest eyes and most innocent looks that I have ever come across. I saw dark terror in the eyes of a North Korean soldier, but that was an isolated incident and I never saw anything of the sort again. The entire trip through North Korea was not anything like I thought it was going to be.

Nothing in DPRK, and I truly mean nothing, was as I had assumed it would be before I arrived.

The mysterious-looking Ryugyong Hotel—a 105-story, 330-meter pyramid-shaped unfinished structure. For 30 years, it has held the title of the Tallest Unoccupied Building In The World.

The four-hour train journey was over quickly because I was very stressed. I had been thinking about the $1.05 worth of North Korean money I managed to get my hands on through trade with one of the merchants. I wanted those currency notes as my own souvenirs of North Korea. But the idea of going to jail over $1.05 was truly a frightening concept. So, I spent a couple of hours wracking my brain, plotting, planning and scheming how to get two North Korean bills out of their country and safely into China...

Summer swimming in a watering hole alongside the railroad line. There are no telephones in North Korea, so that must be a powerline in the swimming hole that is not being used!

Suddenly the train pulled into Sinuiju, the border town just across the river from Dandong, China, and immigration came onto the train. The same immigration officer who had taken my passport when I arrived saw me and said to me with a smile, "Ah, Canada." He was not my immigration officer this time as he was taking care of another section of the train car I was on.

Instead, we got an immigration officer in his late forties, wearing a higher-ranking uniform and hat. He was smiling at one of the tour guides on the train who he had obviously dealt with many times. When he got to us to search our bags, he had a pleasant demeanor. He asked a Chinese girl to open her luggage for him to inspect. As another girl behind him went to move her luggage, it bumped against the immigration officer's leg. He was playful and embellished on the moment, pretending to fall, letting out a yell, and turning around laughing.

It was good-natured and hysterical because it seemed so out of place. When the officer went to search my backpack, he barely looked inside, nodded his head and moved on to the next person. He did not even check my camera.

My North Korea exit form. It asked about currency. It also asked, "Do you have any weapon, ammunition, explosives, killing device? Drug, exciter, narcotics, poison?"

After we had all been cleared by immigration, the train took off again and carried us across the bridge to Dandong, China, where I cleared Chinese immigration with my $1.05 of North Korean currency and a bottle of liquor with a snake in it that a Chinese girl on the train had earlier told me would not be allowed into China. I exited the train station to find Sabrina from Explore North Korea waiting for me to ask about the journey and to get her camera back. She wanted to take me out for dinner before my next train would take me from Dandong to Beijing overnight.

> It is funny how life works. China seemed so strange to me before because of its peculiarities that I am not used to, but after a trip to North Korea, China suddenly felt very familiar.

Everything in China felt a lot brighter than the DPRK somehow. Even standing in the sun felt warmer in China. I guessed that was my subconscious still hanging onto previous prejudices that it did not want to give up in regards to North Korea. Upon returning to China my mind seemed to be tying to maintain alignment with what the media would have us think about North Korea. However, moments later when Sabrina and I walked past a Starbucks, I nearly vomited in my mouth at the sight of capitalist greed. What had I come back to?

Every political system seems to be seriously flawed and I am not convinced that any country has got it right. I had just been in a country where I was looking at what is largely considered to be the worst political system on the planet, and I am no longer convinced of how much worse off the North Koreans are than anyone else. They do not have the freedom to move around like people of the west, but overall they seem pretty content with the life they presented to me.

In any case, no matter what the world is presently selling, a trip through mysterious North Korea is an entire experience that is nothing short of fascinating.

A FEW MORE PHOTOS FROM
EXITING NORTH KOREA:

Kim Il-sung Square.

Pyongyang, atypically busy with traffic.

*Arch of Triumph. Kim Il-sung's gift to his people on his birthday,
a massive arch in commemoration of his 70 years of life.*

Girls practicing dance in front of the Arch of Triumph.

The Pyongyang Television Tower.

*This bus quit working, so the driver's assistant had to get out
and move the electrical lines for better contact.*

*The Monument to the Achievement of China. This monument is in memory
of the Chinese who fought with the Koreans in the war from 1950-1953.*

*Locals waiting for buses in a busy area next to the
Monument to the Achievement of China.*

These trolleys are identical to the ones in Prague, Czech Republic.

Inside of the foreigner's waiting lounge in the Pyongyang train station. After I took this photo, Kim told me I was not allowed to use a camera in the building. On a wall in this room was a photo of North Korea shooting off missiles. The photos were either to mark an achievement, or they were as a reminder to foreigners.

The flame on top of this building is meant to resemble the one on top of Juche Tower. I wanted to ask Kim if this was an ice cream shop, but I did not think he would find that funny.

A North Korean-made three-ton truck.

*Welcome/Farewell North Koreans dressed in
traditional clothes at Pyongyang Station.*

Saying goodbye to Kim.

I am not sure what that building is, but we saw it as we were leaving North Korea.
Had they wanted us to see it, it is certain that they would have shown it to us.

Farmers out working the rice paddies.

*Busy North Koreans. These people work hard and there
are always people everywhere in the countryside.*

I love the wear on the train cars in North Korea. USED EXTENSIVELY. All of them.